Y0-DKC-768

ACTION SCIENCE

SIMPLE CHEMISTRY

Neil Ardley
Series consultant: Professor Eric Laithwaite

Franklin Watts
London   New York   Toronto   Sydney

WITHDRAWN

j540
A69

The author
Neil Ardley gained a degree in science and worked as
a research chemist and patent agent before entering
publishing. He is now a full-time writer and is the
author of more than fifty information books on
science, natural history and music.

The consultant
Eric Laithwaite is Professor of Heavy Electrical
Engineering at Imperial College, London. A well-
known television personality and broadcaster, he is
best known for his inventions on linear motors.

© 1984 Franklin Watts Ltd

First published in Great
Britain in 1984 by
Franklin Watts Ltd
12a Golden Square
London W1

First published in the United
States of America by
Franklin Watts Inc.
387 Park Avenue South
New York
N.Y. 10016

Printed in Belgium

UK edition:
ISBN 0 86313 177 8
US edition:
ISBN 0-531-03778-9
Library of Congress
Catalog Card Number:
83-51444

Designed by
David Jefferis

Illustrated by Janos Marffy,
Hayward Art Group and
Arthur Tims

ACTION SCIENCE

SIMPLE CHEMISTRY

Contents

Equipment

In addition to a few everyday items, you will need the following equipment to carry out the activities in this book. Items with a star may be purchased either at a drugstore or found in a chemistry set.

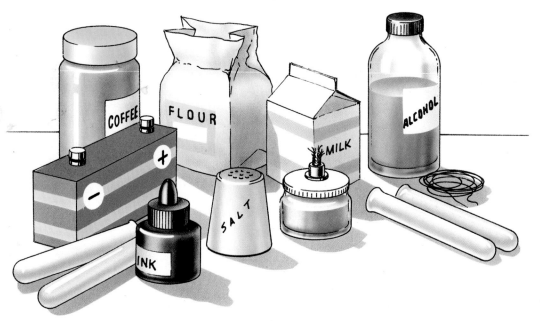

Alcohol
*Alum
Battery (about 3 volts)
Black ink
Bleach
Burner
*Copper sulphate
Electrical wire
Flour and milk
*Hydrogen peroxide
Instant coffee powder

*Iodine solution
  (tincture of iodine)
*Iron filings
Magnet
Salt and sugar
*Sodium bicarbonate
*Sodium carbonate
*Sulphur powder
*Test tubes
*Universal indicator paper
  (or Litmus paper)
Vinegar

Introduction

Our bodies make use of chemistry to provide us with energy. To cook food, we need to apply chemistry. With chemistry, scientists can make new substances such as plastics, dyes of all colors and drugs to fight disease and pain. Yet all these things are done by the action of tiny molecules far too small to be seen except in the most powerful microscopes.

By doing the activities in this book, you will begin to find out how chemistry works. You will see how substances react together to give new and different substances. There are exciting experiments to do, such as making your own plastics and gases, electroplating objects and forming brilliant colors.

Before you start, read the section about safety on page 31 to find out how to carry out the experiments properly. Take care and remember this advice at all times.

✷ This symbol appears throughout the book. It shows you where to find the scientific explanation for the results of an experiment.

Different liquids dissolve different substances.

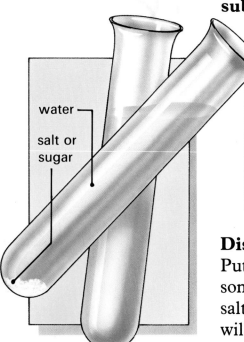

water

salt or sugar

Heat the top of the liquid.

Use a paper holder.

△ You can taste the solution to check that the salt or sugar has not vanished. Heating makes molecules move faster so more salt or sugar dissolves in hot water. However, the water can get so full of salt or sugar molecules that it will hold no more and no more salt or sugar will dissolve.

Dissolving in water

Put some cold water in a test tube and add some salt. Shake the tube to dissolve the salt. Add more salt to find out how much will dissolve in the water. Heat the tube and notice that more salt dissolves in warm water. Try again with sugar instead of salt. Much more sugar dissolves than salt.

✸ A substance such as salt or sugar dissolves in a liquid like water and makes a solution. Tiny invisible particles called molecules in the liquid invade the substance. The liquid molecules pull the molecules in the substance apart so that the substance seems to disappear into the water as the solution forms.

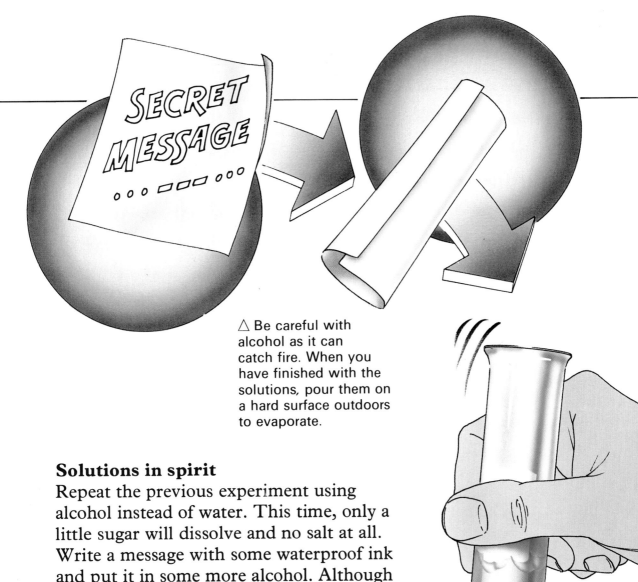

△ Be careful with alcohol as it can catch fire. When you have finished with the solutions, pour them on a hard surface outdoors to evaporate.

Solutions in spirit

Repeat the previous experiment using alcohol instead of water. This time, only a little sugar will dissolve and no salt at all. Write a message with some waterproof ink and put it in some more alcohol. Although the ink is waterproof, the writing may gradually disappear!

✷ Alcohol has different molecules than water. They cannot invade salt but can get into sugar to form a solution. The molecules make the dyes in the ink dissolve easily, so the message vanishes.

7

Coffee and crystals

Pure substances can be obtained from solutions.

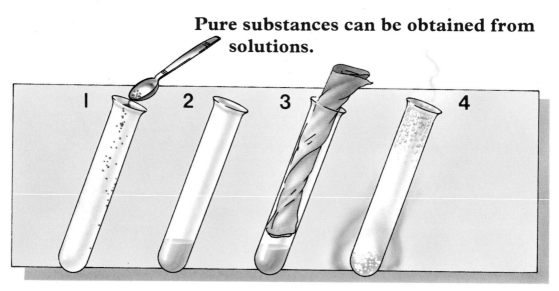

△ If you do not have any instant coffee, use a little salt instead.

Distil some water

Put a few grains of instant coffee in a tube and add a little water. Dry the inside walls of the tube above the coffee with a twist of tissue. Heat the tube so that the coffee boils. Drops of water form at the top of the tube. Allow the tube to cool and taste this water. It contains no coffee at all.

✳ The coffee in the tube is a solution of coffee in water. When it boils, the coffee stays in the solution. Some water leaves the solution as steam. It then forms pure water at the top of the tube where it is cool. This process is called distillation. It is used to make pure water from sea water.

Grow a crystal

Dissolve some alum in hot water. Add more alum until no more will dissolve. Pour off the clear solution into a glass. Next suspend a small alum crystal in the solution and cover the glass. Over the next few days, a large eight-sided alum crystal will grow.

☀ Water gradually disappears from the solution as water vapor. The water remaining in the glass cannot hold all the alum molecules that are in it, so they begin to leave the solution. These alum molecules join themselves to the alum molecules in the small crystal, making the crystal grow.

▽ Molecules line up in rows as they join together to form crystals. This is why a crystal grows in a particular shape.

Handling mixtures

Substances that are mixed together can be separated.

Separate a mixture

Take equal quantities of salt and flour and stir them together in a bowl to produce a white powder. Note that you cannot see the individual salt crystals or flour grains. Add some hot water to the bowl. Stir and allow the powder to settle. Dip your finger into the water and taste it. The salt has gone into the water and the flour is left at the bottom of the bowl.

▷ Taste a little flour and salt before you mix them. You will then be able to identify them later.

✹ The salt crystals in the mixture dissolve in the water, but the flour does not. Mixtures of substances that dissolve differently can be separated in this way.

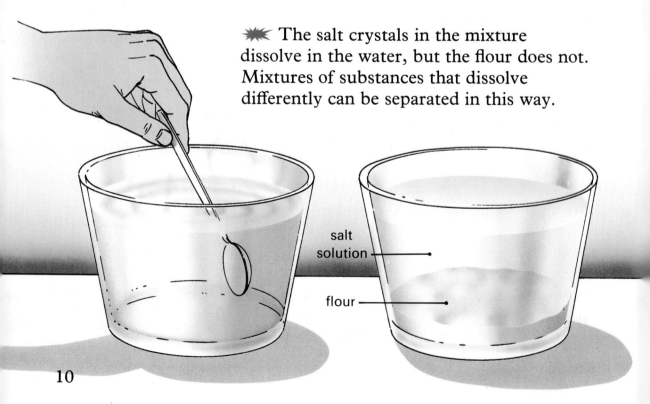

salt solution

flour

10

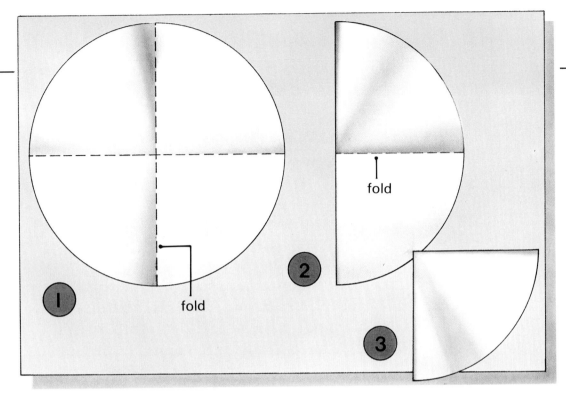

1

2 fold

3 fold

Purify the products

Continue the last experiment. Make a filter as shown and wet it. Then pour in the salty water and flour, and collect the water in a container. Next let a little hot water drip through the filter. Spread out the paper and leave it to dry. You will get back the flour that went into the mixture. To get the salt, boil the water in a pan until the water evaporates.

✳ The grains of flour are too big to go through the fine holes in the filter. They remain on the paper while the salt solution passes through it. Adding the hot water removes any salt still in the flour.

△ To make a filter, cut a circle of absorbent paper. Fold it into a cone and place it in a funnel.

Elements and compounds

Sulphur floats.

Iron filings sink.

△ A mixture of iron filings and sulphur easily separates in water.

▽ Burning sulphur has a choking smell, so open windows or the door to get some fresh air.

Chemical compounds are made by combining different elements.

Iron and sulphur

Mix two parts of iron filings and three of sulphur powder. Take a little of the mixture and separate it with a magnet or in water. Only the iron filings are magnetic and only the sulphur floats. Now heat the mixture strongly. It melts and turns into a black substance. Allow it to cool. The substance is not magnetic and does not float.

✸ Iron and sulphur are elements. When heated, they form a chemical compound called iron sulphide. The black substance is this compound. In a compound, elements are held together very strongly and cannot be separated like a mixture.

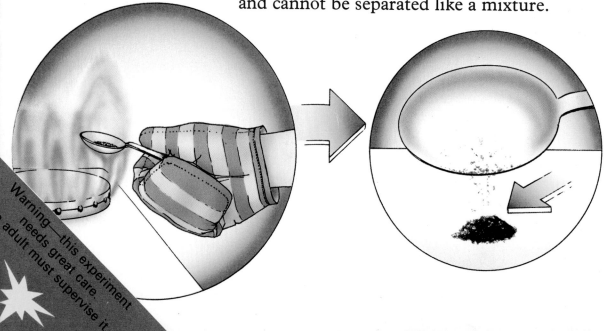

Warning—this experiment needs great care. An adult must supervise it.

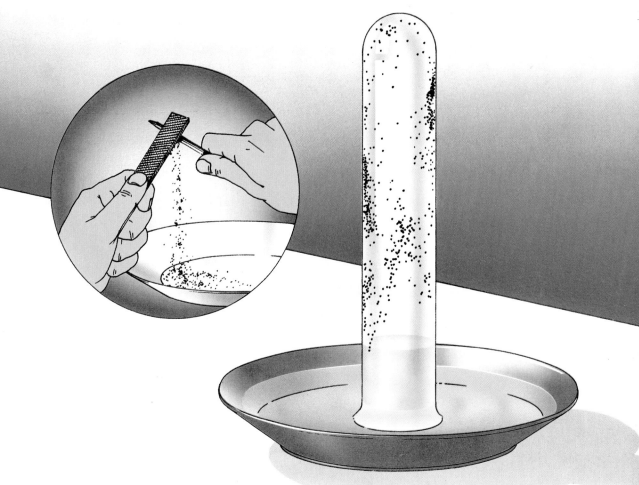

Iron and oxygen

Take a wet tube and sprinkle a few iron
filings inside. Place the tube upsidedown
in some water and leave it for a few hours.
The water rises a short distance up the
tube and the iron filings go brown.

△ Iron filings can be
made by scraping a
piece of iron such as a
large nail with a file.

✳ Iron combines with oxygen, which is
another element present as a gas in air.
The iron filings remove oxygen from the
air in the tube. The pressure of the air
outside pushes some water up the tube to
replace this oxygen. Iron and oxygen
combine to form iron oxide, which is rust.
This is why the filings go brown.

13

Making elements

iron filings

Elements can be released from their compounds by chemical reactions.

△ A chemical reaction occurs between the iron filings and the acid in the vinegar. These substances change to produce hydrogen and other substances. Reactions usually go faster if the substances are heated; warming the tube gives more bubbles of hydrogen.

Making hydrogen

Take two tubes. Dissolve a few crystals of copper sulphate in a little warm water in one tube. Place some iron filings in the other and half fill it with vinegar. Add a few drops of the copper sulphate solution. Bubbles begin to form. Put your thumb over the tube until you can feel the gas inside pressing on it. Bring a lighted match up to the mouth of the tube and remove your thumb. You should hear a loud pop.

✳ Vinegar is an acid (a compound containing the element hydrogen). Iron, helped by the copper sulphate, releases hydrogen gas from the acid. It builds up in the tube, then burns to give the pop.

14

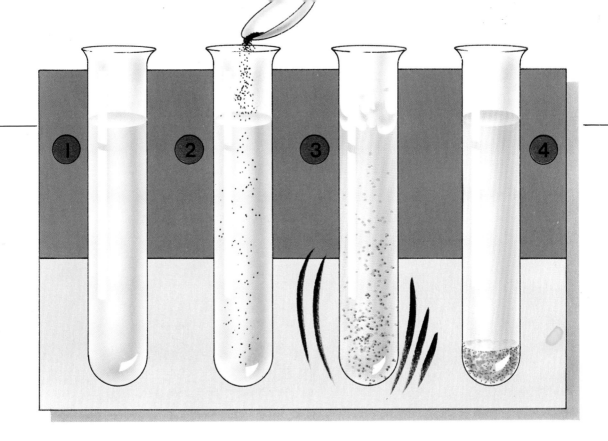

Turn iron into copper

Half fill a tube with blue copper sulphate solution (1). Then add some black iron filings (2). Put your thumb over the end of the tube and shake it hard (3). The filings turn red-brown and the solution changes to pale green (4).

✳ The iron molecules attack the molecules of copper sulphate in the solution. They break up the copper sulphate, which is a compound containing copper and sulphur. This produces a solution of iron sulphate, which is green. The copper, which is a red-brown element, is forced out of the solution and falls to the bottom of the tube.

△ This experiment works because iron is an element that forms compounds more readily than copper does. The two elements change places with each other, iron freeing copper from the copper sulphate and taking its place to form iron sulphate.

Several elements, including metals such as gold and silver, can be made from minerals in this way. Minerals are compounds of elements that are found in the ground, often in rocks. Sea water also contains some dissolved minerals.

15

Changing compounds

Chemical reactions will change one compound into another if possible.

△ You can use Epsom salt and water instead of sodium bicarbonate and vinegar. This is because the salt contains sodium bicarbonate and an acid. When the salts dissolve, the acid attacks the bicarbonate in the same way as vinegar, releasing carbon dioxide.

Forming gases from solids

Place some sodium bicarbonate in a glass and add some vinegar. The bicarbonate and vinegar immediately begin to fizz. Light a match and lower it into the glass. The flame is suddenly snuffed out!

✴ Sodium bicarbonate is a compound containing the elements sodium, hydrogen, carbon and oxygen. The acid in the vinegar attacks this compound. It makes the carbon and oxygen link to form another compound called carbon dioxide. This is a gas and it stays in the glass. The match goes out as soon as it enters the carbon dioxide.

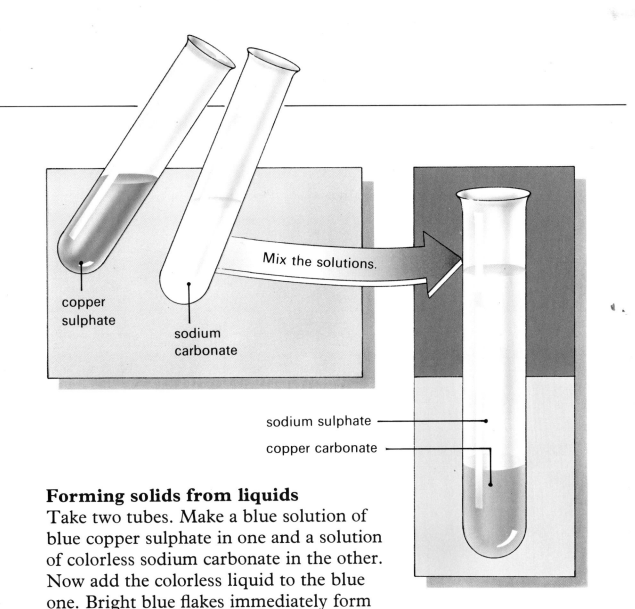

copper
sulphate

sodium
carbonate

Mix the solutions.

sodium sulphate

copper carbonate

Forming solids from liquids

Take two tubes. Make a blue solution of
blue copper sulphate in one and a solution
of colorless sodium carbonate in the other.
Now add the colorless liquid to the blue
one. Bright blue flakes immediately form
and settle to the bottom of the tube.

When mixed in solutions, the two
compounds react together and exchange
elements. The blue flakes are made of
copper carbonate. This cannot dissolve in
water. Sodium sulphate is also formed, but
it is colorless and stays dissolved.

△ When the compounds
dissolve in water, their
molecules split to give
copper, sodium,
carbonate and sulphate
particles. A chemical
reaction occurs because
the particles can then
link to form different
compounds.

17

Using heat

How does heat affect substances and reactions?

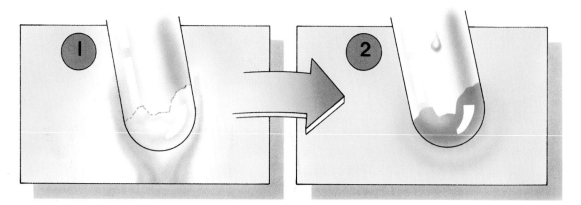

△ Some reactions, such as cooking, need heat to work; others give out heat, like burning. Copper sulphate and water are unusual because they can produce both kinds of reactions.

Color changes

Place a few crystals of blue copper sulphate in a clean, dry tube. Hold the tube at an angle and heat the base. The crystals go white and droplets of water form at the top of the tube. Let the tube cool. Hold it by the base and add a drop of water. The crystals turn blue, and the tube gets hot.

✻ Blue copper sulphate crystals contain water molecules. When heated, the crystals take up heat energy which drives out this water. When they lose water, the crystals go white. But when water is added, its molecules go back into the crystals, turning them blue. The energy that was taken up is now set free, giving out heat.

Sizzling sugar

Put some sugar into an old spoon and hold it over a flame. Steam comes off as the sugar begins to melt to a brown-black liquid, and the sugar then catches fire. After burning, a hard black crust is left.

✳ Sugar is a compound of carbon, hydrogen and oxygen. When heated, the hydrogen and oxygen combine to produce water. This escapes, leaving black carbon behind. Then the carbon begins to combine with oxygen in the air, giving out heat as the sugar burns.

△ The sugar behaves like fuels such as coal or wood, which burn because they react with oxygen to give out heat. Unlike the copper sulphate in the previous experiment, the reaction will not go the other way and give the sugar or fuels again.

19

PLEASANT HILLS PUBLIC LIBRARY

Electrical effects

▽ Fix a piece of pencil lead to a wire and connect it to the positive (+) terminal of a battery. Attach some aluminum foil to another wire. Connect this to the negative (−) terminal. Place the wires inside two upsidedown tubes in salt solution.

Electricity can break compounds apart.

Splitting salt
Set up the apparatus shown. Bubbles of gas rise in the tubes. When the tube containing the foil is about half full, place your thumb over the top and remove it from the salt solution. Test the gas with a match. It pops. Test the other gas by sniffing it. It smells like a swimming pool.

✳ The first gas is hydrogen, which burns with a pop, and the second is chlorine. They are formed because the electricity splits the salt in the water. Salt is a compound of the elements sodium and chlorine. Bubbles of chlorine form in one tube. Sodium forms in the other and reacts with the water to produce hydrogen.

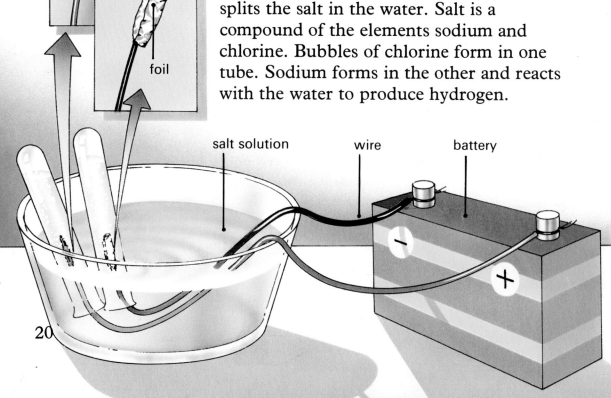

tape

pencil lead

foil

salt solution   wire   battery

△ Connect the silver coin to the negative terminal of the battery, and the copper coin to the positive terminal. Make sure that the coins do not touch in the solution.

Curious coin

Take a silver coin and a copper coin. Tape them to electrical wire and attach the wires to a battery as shown. Put the coins in copper sulphate solution for a few minutes. The silver coin turns into a copper coin, but the copper coin is not affected.

✳ The copper sulphate molecules split into copper and sulphate particles in the water. The electric current pulls the copper particles to the silver coin, giving it a copper surface where it is exposed to the solution. The sulphate particles go to the copper coin. There they join with some copper to make more copper sulphate.

△ Coating articles with metals like this is called electroplating. It produces a very thin but very firm coating of metal that cannot be rubbed off.

21

Warning—this experiment needs great care. An adult must supervise it.

Chemical testing

Color changes produced by chemical reactions can identify substances.

▷ Wash the nail or screw before using it, and hold the end in a cloth or glove.

▽ Fireworks contain metal compounds to give bright colors to flares and stars. Strontium compounds give a deep red and barium compounds a light green.

Flame test

Take a long steel nail or screw, wet the end and dip it in some salt. Place it in a gas flame, and the flame will turn bright yellow-orange. Try dipping it in copper sulphate. This time it goes green-blue. Try other substances that do not burn to see if they will color the flame.

✸ The flame test works if the substances or solutions being tested contain compounds of certain metals. Each metal gives a different color. Sodium compounds color the flame yellow-orange, copper compounds produce green-blue, calcium compounds red-yellow and potassium compounds give a lilac color.

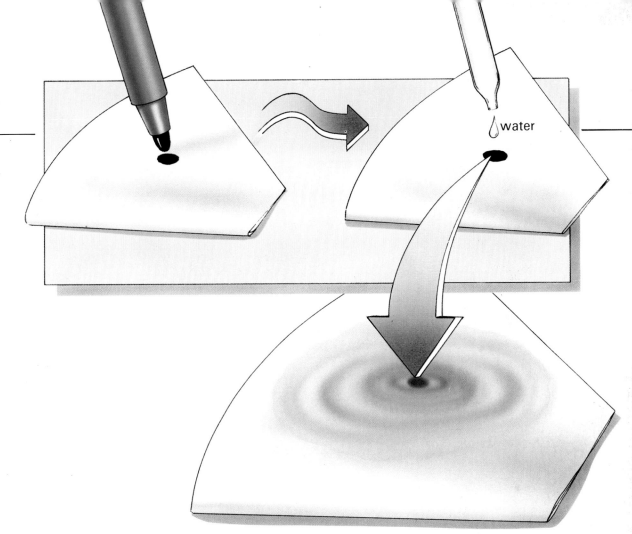

Separating dyes

Take a piece of absorbent paper. Put a drop of black ink in the middle or mark the paper with a black felt-tip pen. When the ink has stopped spreading, add a few drops of water in the same place. The ink spreads out much more, separating into rings of different colors.

✴ The black ink is a mixture of several colored dyes. The water carries the dyes as it spreads through the paper, and the various dyes move different distances.

△ Filter paper or filter bags used for making coffee work well for this test. Try different colored inks and liquids to find out if they are mixtures of colors or not. This kind of testing is called chromatography. It is very important in chemistry for detecting unknown substances.

Continued overpage

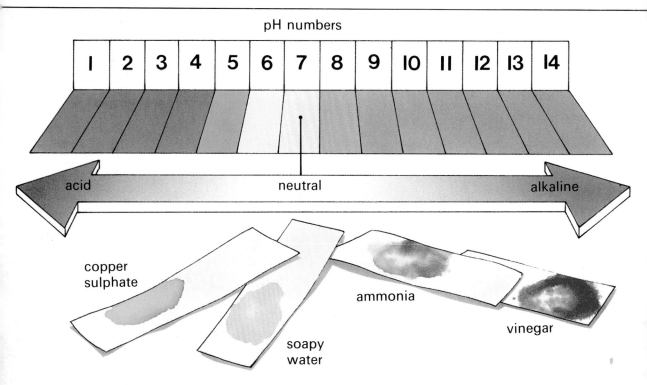

pH numbers

| 1 | 2 | 3 | 4 | 5 | 6 | 7 | 8 | 9 | 10 | 11 | 12 | 13 | 14 |

acid   neutral   alkaline

copper sulphate

soapy water

ammonia

vinegar

△ Testing with indicators is important in detecting substances. Indicator paper contains dyes which change color in acids and alkalis. The colour indicates the pH number, which shows how strong the acid or alkali is. Try to get litmus paper if you cannot obtain universal indicator paper. Litmus turns red in acids and blue in alkalis.

Universal indicator

Take some universal indicator paper, which has a dark yellow color. Using a dropper, put drops of different liquids or solutions on the paper. Some make the paper go red or orange, while others produce a blue or purple color.

✸ The color indicates whether the liquid or solution is acid or alkaline. Vinegar, which is acid, gives an orange-red colour. Soapy water is alkaline and makes the indicator go green-blue. Strong acids or alkalis give deep colors.

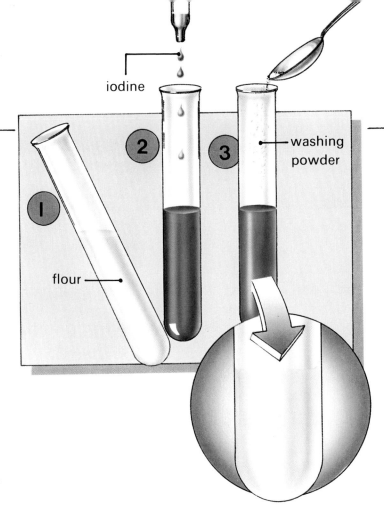

iodine

2

3

1

flour

washing
powder

▽ Add only a drop or
two of the iodine
solution. Iodine solution
(tincture of iodine) can
be purchased at
drugstores. Test various
kinds of food to see if
they contain starch.
Throw the food away
afterwards.

Starch detector

Put some flour in a tube and add some
water (1). Stir the contents and add some
iodine solution (2). The flour goes deep
blue. Now stir in some biological detergent
(3). The blue color slowly fades.

✳ Iodine gives a blue color with starch,
which is present in many foods and
ingredients such as flour. Iodine can detect
very small amounts of starch. Biological
detergent contains enzymes which
destroy starch and cause the blue color
to disappear.

25

Producing plastics

Make some plastics and shape them into objects.

▽ The first plastic was made from natural sources such as milk and plants. Now plastic is produced from chemicals that come from oil. But they all have long molecules like casein made from milk.

Molding with milk

Place half a cup of milk in a pan and warm it. Then stir in some vinegar. A white rubbery material forms. Take this out, wash it under the tap and shape it into objects such as counters. Leave them for a few days, and the material will harden.

✳ The vinegar and milk react to give casein. Molecules of protein in the milk join together to give molecules of casein, which are so long that they can bend, making the casein rubbery. Then the casein molecules join together, making it hard.

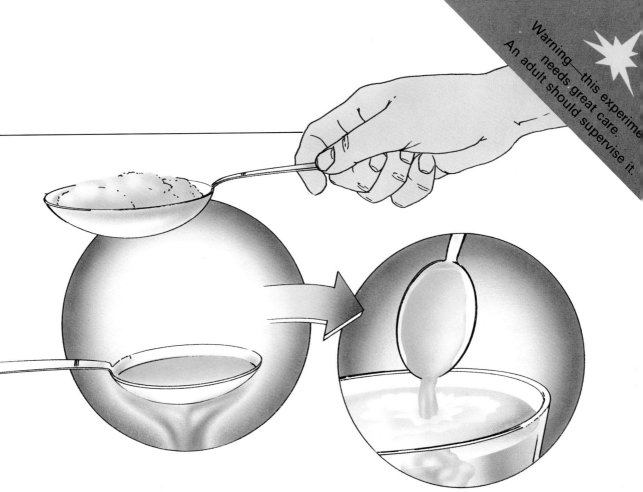

Warning—this experiment needs great care. An adult should supervise it.

Plastic sulphur

Place some sulphur powder in a metal container such as a spoon and warm it. The sulphur melts to a brown liquid. Immediately pour the liquid sulphur into some cold water. It gives a rubbery substance that you can shape into objects. The plastic sulphur sets in a few minutes.

△ Use a spoon or container that you do not want as it will be coated in sulphur afterwards. Do this experiment in a place with plenty of air as the sulphur may begin to burn with a choking smell.

✴ Treating the sulphur in this way causes its molecules to join together in long chains that can twist and stretch, making it rubbery. The chains then soon change into ring-shaped molecules, and the plastic sulphur goes hard.

sulphur disc

Warning—this experiment needs great care. An adult should supervise it.

Home chemistry

Cooking and bleaching are just two everyday uses of chemistry.

Make some toffee
Take the ingredients shown. Melt the butter in the pan and add the syrup and sugar. Stir until the mixture boils, then continue boiling for about 12 minutes. Pour the mixture into a tin greased with butter. It sets hard to make toffee.

✳ The compounds in the syrup, butter and sugar react together when heated to produce the toffee. All cooking consists of chemical reactions like this, but they have to be controlled. Overcooking and burning happen if the reactions go too far.

TOFFEE RECIPE

¼ lb Butter
1 lb Corn Syrup
1 lb Brown Sugar

△ The pan will be sticky and hard to clean afterwards. Put some hot water in it and leave the pan for a few hours before washing it.

sulphur

foil

hydrogen peroxide

Turn a flower white

Take a colored flower such as a red rose and tape it to the side of a glass. Put some sulphur powder on some foil, light it and place the glass over the burning sulphur. Watch the flower. It goes white. Now take the flower out of the glass and dip it in some hydrogen peroxide. The color comes back!

✳ Sulphur burns and gives off sulphur dioxide gas, which bleaches the flower. It takes oxygen from the colored substance in the flower, changing it to a white substance. The hydrogen peroxide restores the oxygen in the substance.

△ Do this experiment where there is plenty of air because sulphur dioxide has a choking smell. Other substances can bleach colors in addition to sulphur dioxide. In the home, solutions containing chlorine are often used as well as hydrogen peroxide.

More about chemistry

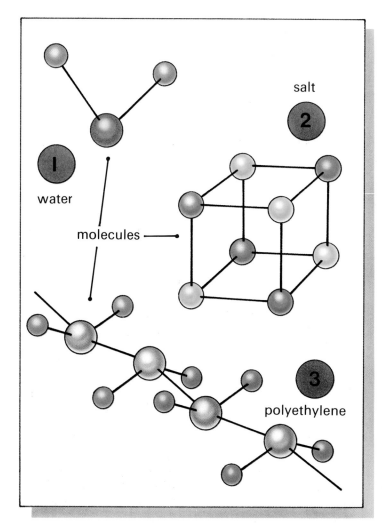

1 water
molecules ⟶
2 salt
3 polyethylene

△ The atoms in these molecules are hydrogen (blue), oxygen (red), sodium (yellow), chlorine (green) and carbon (black).

Atoms and molecules
All substances are made up of millions and millions of tiny atoms. Atoms are tiny particles of elements. In most substances, the atoms form small groups called molecules. If the substance is pure, all the molecules contain the same kinds of atoms. In pure water, for example, each molecule is made of two hydrogen atoms and one oxygen atom.

Chemical reactions
When a chemical reaction happens, two or more elements or compounds come together and exchange atoms between them. Their molecules break apart and new molecules are formed, producing different elements or compounds.

Compounds
Compounds are substances that have molecules in which there are atoms of two or more elements. Salt, for example, is a compound of the elements sodium and chlorine. It is called sodium chloride in chemistry.

Crystals
Crystals are solid

elements or compounds in which the atoms or molecules are all arranged in rows to form patterns. The pattern of rows may give a crystal a particular shape. Salt crystals form cubes, for example.

Elements

Elements are substances in which all the atoms are the same. About 100 different elements exist. They include hydrogen, oxygen, iron, aluminum, copper, chlorine, iodine, sulphur, carbon, sodium and calcium. A few more can be made by scientists.

Safety tips

1. Take care not to burn or scald yourself when heating anything.
2. Put out burning matches or glowing splints when you have finished with them.
3. Use a spirit burner for heating if possible, otherwise a candle. You may need a gas flame for strong heating.
4. When you heat liquids

Keep your face away

Point the tube away from yourself and others.

Use a holder; it can be made of paper.

burner

in a tube, heat the top part of the liquid.
5. Keep your eyes away from experiments and **never** taste chemicals.
6. If you spill any chemicals, wipe them up right away with a damp cloth and wash out the cloth.
7. After an experiment, wash the chemicals down the sink with lots of water. Wash your hands to remove any chemicals.
8. Label bottles and always put tops back on. Store chemicals so that they are out of the reach

△ This is how you should heat a tube.

of young children, and keep your chemistry equipment separate from household objects.

Substances

Substances are the things of which objects and materials are made. Water, milk, glass, air, steel and salt are all substances, for example. Substances consist of elements or compounds, either on their own or mixed with other elements or compounds.

Index